T0058472

Exposing Phallacy

Flashing In Contemporary Culture

Exposing Phallacy

Flashing In Contemporary Culture

Kate Gould

Winchester, UK
Washington, USA

First published by Zero Books, 2012
Zero Books is an imprint of John Hunt Publishing Ltd., Laurel House, Station Approach,
Alresford, Hants, SO24 9JH, UK
office1@o-books.net
www.o-books.com

For distributor details and how to order please visit the 'Ordering' section on our website.

Text copyright: Kate Gould 2011

ISBN: 978 1 84694 964 7

All rights reserved. Except for brief quotations in critical articles or reviews, no part of this
book may be reproduced in any manner without prior written permission from the publishers.

The rights of Kate Gould as author have been asserted in accordance with the Copyright, Designs
and Patents Act 1988.

A CIP catalogue record for this book is available from the British Library.

Design: Stuart Davies

Printed and bound by CPI Group (UK) Ltd, Croydon, CR0 4YY
Printed in the USA by Offset Paperback Mfrs, Inc

We operate a distinctive and ethical publishing philosophy in all
areas of our business, from our global network of authors to
production and worldwide distribution.

CONTENTS

For beautiful, bright, beloved Em. I didn't tell you enough.

The Irresistible Urge

I feel somewhat indebted to flashers. Without them, my grandparents might never have met, and I would not have been born. My grandfather was a policeman, involved in the investigation into a man who repeatedly contravened the blackout regulations of World War II by opening his coat and shining a torch on his exposed penis. My grandmother was conscripted as bait in an attempt to lure the man into exposing himself to her, while my grandfather and several other policemen hid in the bushes, ready to spring out and apprehend him. Not the most romantic of beginnings. And, though I'm sure it was through no lack of allurement on my grandmother's part, they didn't catch the man.

I'm taking a slightly different approach to apprehending flashers. Rather than put them in manacles, I've got them to talk about what they do and why. I've spent time in online forums and chat rooms, reading their tales and seeing their revealing, to say the least, pictures. I've learnt a thing or two about how best to flash if you don't want to get caught (skirts that accidentally blow up for women and lycra shorts for men – you get the exposure but have the defense of being fully clothed should anyone object). I've spoken to women who've been flashed to find out how they reacted and why. I've been introduced to sexual practices I never knew existed and seen attitudes expressed of which I was only too well aware. There are no easy conclusions to be drawn about flashers and their urge to expose, as there are no easy conclusions to be drawn about any aspect of human behavior, but I've tried to draw out some sense of what they do, what it means and why.

One of the many things that have struck me is that we are all exhibitionists, whether sporting an enormous ostrich feathered hat, leopard print jumpsuit, and neon pink platform moon boots or adding a brooch, earrings or cufflinks to a navy work suit. We decide how much of our bodies to show, displaying the cleavage (breasts and buttocks) of which we are so proud, the legs hours in the gym have toned almost to rigidity, our faces glowing with the spray-on tan that never fades. Or we effect nonchalance in jeans and t-shirt which, in itself, makes a statement. Then we add mannerisms and movement. We create spectacles with our bodies, using them to convey an image of how we want to be perceived. The man in his jumpsuit, hat, and boots or the teenage girl in hot pants, push-up bra, and tiny Playboy-branded t-shirt are deliberately creating that image – the man wants you to know he's flamboyant and the girl wants you to know that she thinks she's sexy. For most of us, it isn't quite as conscious or the result so conspicuous, but every morning we dress our bodies to communicate something of who we are.

The difference between flashers and non-flashers is that, to a flasher, exhibitionism is the use of the naked body, specifically the genitals, to communicate. For a male flasher, it is the magnificence of his penis (as he sees it) that he wishes to display. His sexual gratification is obtained from the fact that, regardless of how the person he flashes reacts, his penis is worthy of attention and, in all his naked glory, he commands a response. The female flasher seeks approval and appreciation from a male audience. Men applauding at the sight of her naked vagina make her feel sexy and desired, regardless of whether she finds them attractive or would actually want to go anywhere near them.

To flash is an urge they are unable to resist, despite the fact that they're risking arrest, imprisonment, registration as sex offenders, and loss of their homes, children, relationships, jobs, and freedom. It's more than just a little kink to spice up their sex lives.

For all the male flasher may plead otherwise, saying it's just a little fun and he doesn't want to upset women, his flashing is an aggressive act. It invades the woman's space, forces her into a confrontation, and makes her afraid. He has greater right to that space than she, he believes, and refuses to understand why no one, besides the fellow flashers he meets in online forums, joins him in his cock worship.

The female flasher, with her shaved vagina, puts on a porn-esque performance for men to convince them (and herself, if she were to admit it) that she is sexy, desirable, and naughty. Mimicking the moves of the porn stars in the soft porn culture that surrounds her, she bends, poses, and moans, splaying her legs in front of webcams and sharing her flashing experiences with men ravenous for details so they can imagine themselves in the scenarios and brag to her about how hard they came thinking of them.

By way of introduction, this gives you a peek into life as flashers know it. In the process of exploring it, I've become enraged, horrified, despairing, fascinated, and bewildered. See what you make of it.

Slick Slits and Throbbing Clits

Female flashers are a brazen lot. Sharing their accounts of flashing experiences and pictures on exhibitionist forums, they tell of cycling without underwear to 'accidentally' flash men; teasing teenagers in shops with glimpses of their vaginas, contriving to make it appear accidental by bending over to look through racks of books; they lie with legs splayed and vaginas shaved at nudist resorts; post pictures of themselves in chat rooms, their backs to the camera, bent over to reveal their vaginas; press their breasts against the camera, imploring men to show their appreciation by clicking on the 'like' button and delighting in comments about them shooting their load thinking about what they want to do to them; they leave the house naked, hiding when they encounter a man; wear skirts that blow up in the wind and loose tops that fall open when they lean forward. Some begin as children, enjoying being looked at by male relatives and parents' friends. They arrange meetings with strangers to watch each other masturbate in the back of cars; campaign bare-breasted for the same right as men to be topless in public; and fantasize about being locked outside, naked, and about men watching and getting turned on by them masturbating in public.

It's an exciting experience, a turn-on and an urge on which they feel compelled to act. The talk is of "slick slits" and "throbbing clits". As a presentation of female sexuality, it bypasses the dabbling in soft porn so rampant in our culture and moves straight on to hardcore. There is no posing in Playboy t-shirts with breasts pushed up and jeans worn low to reveal g-strings; no glossed lips or tottering in heels wearing get-up said to be empowering by girls, sexualized at an increasingly young age, who have little real idea of the implications of their actions and are unlikely to be able to handle the situations in which their clothing and posturing may place them. These girls' references are perkily plastic Barbie's replacement, the Jenna Jameson doll (with removable clothes no less), modeled on a woman whose fortune has been made faking it – from her breasts to her orgasms. Pornography is not only ubiquitous; it has become a standard against which sexiness is measured. Over 3000 women auditioned for positions as bunnies in the London Playboy Club, opened in May 2011; Ann Summers, with its crotchless knickers and cheerleader outfits, had a turnover of £117.3 million in 2007-08. Images of women, lust faked for the camera, are on the shelves of every supermarket - the trout pout is ridiculed, but plumped lips are a staple in the illusion of agelessness, and women's magazines encourage a pornesque performance in the bedroom. But these plays on pornography don't actually have anything to do with sex. They are the props of sexual desire, ersatz and a caricature of lust and sexiness, sexy but not sexual. Their enduring appeal is based on the ease with which they can be performed and their distance from the physicality of sex. Like the depiction of sex in mainstream cinema, the one thing conspicuously absent is genitals. There is no cunnilingus in Hollywood.

The female body is not what's on display. It is closer to the plastic of the Jenna Jameson figurine than to the flesh. This is not female sexuality. There is no life in these dull-eyed porn star clones; nor is there any suggestion that they are there for anything but the titillation of men. They are a plasticized circus of silicon, collagen, and hairlessness; their act a desperate bid to be what their lad mag culture would have them believe is the ultimate male fantasy. From the handful of women made famous by pornography – the porn stars – they believe this is what men want and, therefore, what they should want and try to provide. This emulation ignores the reality of the lives of women degraded and dehumanized in the pornography industry, but it is a significant step towards accepting such treatment of women and seeing it as natural.

We assimilate it into our lives gradually – or in a surge, if the spread of soft porn culture into mainstream is anything to go by. Women endeavor to meet the requirements of what they are led to believe is sexy. They imitate the demeanor and moves of women paid to put on a show. Pole dancing has become a fitness fad, moving out of strip clubs and into the gym. Women emulating and watching female strippers is taken to be rebellious and liberating. Speak to any stripper and the reality is anything but. They tell of being gang raped by men who took their routines to be a come-on. They are strained mentally as well as physically, struggling not to see themselves as the men see them – as nothing more than an object for their pleasure or someone "not worth spitting on", as one woman phrased it. Some talk of an initial excitement when they begin their careers – the thrill of putting on a show – but it quickly fades and the money becomes the only appealing aspect of the job. Women do it to pay off debts, support their families, pay for a drug habit, start their own businesses, or because there are no other jobs available to them. There is no mention of sexual pleasure. That side of stripping is faked and the more convincingly so, the more popular the woman will be. Men give higher tips to women who look like they're enjoying it than to ones who may be more attractive but don't appear to be loving every minute. The woman's pleasure is irrelevant to the spectator. What is important is her ability to create a simulacrum of it. Faking pleasure is something women do too well and too often.

Our culture has taken on the get-up and fakery of the porn star; it has allowed porn's damaging attitudes towards and expectations of women to be trumpeted by the lad mag phenomenon as though it were an acceptable norm. What it hasn't taken on is the vagina. We can totter, pout, read up on how to finesse our blow-job skills, and risk loss of nipple sensation, permanent disfigurement and death for enlarged breasts. What we cannot do publicly, by law and culture, is show our vaginas.

By inviting men to look at their vaginas, female flashers aren't parading these fripperies of femininity: they are confronting men with their femaleness. Though they are used to market everything from cars to politics (think of 'Blair's Babes), images of women's bodies have become normalized to the extent that the use of them for this is almost socially invisible. Purposeful display of her vagina by a woman seeks to re-value what has been socially trans-lated into an entity that harbors only commercial worth. It is an overt display, utterly indulgent and an assertion of her own sexual desires. "Look," she says. "This is my cunt in all its slick, throbbing, fleshly glory. You'll love it like I do and I'll come thinking of the hard-on it's giving you. But you can't have it." Surrounded by an epidemic of faking it for the boys, she has the power and the audacity to show the passion of her sexual hunger. It's the ultimate in female sexual expression, of a woman knowing the power of her body and experiencing the full potency of her desires. Or is it?

Though there are many complexities bound up in female flashers' desire to expose, the single characteristic evident in all their accounts is the enjoyment of male attention. It is both a mental and physical pleasure: the thrill of what they're doing and the sexual gratification they receive from it. Such gratification could not be obtained without the participation of the male audience. If you're putting on a show, there's no point playing to an empty theatre. That is all these women are doing: offering themselves up as spectacles. Though it would seem that they are proud of their bodies, enamored of their own femaleness, what they are in love with is the male attention they receive from it. There is no autonomy in this expression of a woman's sexuality. This is not a woman liberated of the concerns of public decency and societal constraints on sexual expression. She has not freed herself from the bondage of what is expected of her in any meaningful sense and her liberation is no more complete than that of a girl, in g-string and padded bra, in thrall to a porn star.

The women choose to take off their underwear, but that is the single aspect of the situation over which they have any control. Everything else is controlled by the men to whom they display their vaginas. Gaining their attention is the reason for performing the act, it is their approval and appreciation that is sought, and it is around the unpredictable nature of their response – whether it is likely to be praise or attack – that the woman plans her exposure. They all refer to the need to feel safe and of considering the potential consequences before exposing themselves, preferring to do so at crowded beaches or while on a bike or in a car so they can quickly escape if necessary. Some flash while with partners who offer protection, but are there primarily because they enjoy the experience of seeing them expose their vaginas to strangers.

The woman may tell herself it is empowering, sharing the beauty of her form with another, but this is not empowerment; it is objectification. The woman wields no power over her audience. She may feel the breeze between her legs and get off on the response she receives – or perceives

– from the men to whom she exposes, but she still lives within the confines of male approval and male threat. Both on an individual and societal level, it is the man who benefits from the female flasher's exposure. The pleasure she gains from the act is fleeting; the relegation of woman to an object for consumption endemic in our culture that it reinforces is permanent.

As well as being rife, this relegation is highly lucrative. Around £2000 a second is spent on online pornography; men's magazines, most of which use women's bodies displayed in content and advertising, have an annual revenue of just under £75 million in the UK alone, with models receiving £200-£300 per shoot; and British pornographic magazines bring in a further £13.2 million annually, selling around 1.1 million copies each month.

Though they may consider themselves subversive (or just naughty), female flashers emulate the women in porn and posing in lad mags by shaving their vaginas both to be more revealing and because they think men find female pubic hair unpalatable at best and repellent at worst. The comments made in exhibitionist forums by men assessing women's pictures support this view. Like the enormously aggrandized glimpse of Sharon Stone's bald vagina in Basic Instinct (a part for which she received £310,000 while the film grossed £219,000,000 worldwide in cinema sales alone), it is only pink flesh that is to be seen. Unlike Stone's flash, pubic hair in Hollywood might actually have been worth commenting on.

What is displayed is, of course, the vagina of a child – clean, tight, and virginal. As well as the anatomy, the female flasher displays the behavior of a child. She craves male attention and approval, but like a naughty girl, she cannot help behaving badly, whipping up her skirt, waiting for a reaction, then running away. She is, at once, infantilized and sexualized, a curious chimera of woman and child, trying desperately to seduce her male audience. They are who she is empowering. She is simply an object for them to leer at and discard.

The Penis And Masculinity

Cock, knob, chopper, dick, tool, prick, joystick, one-eyed monster, family jewels, shaft, whang, member, organ, John Thomas, weenie, dong, plonker, meat, schlong, pecker, willy, phallus, tadger, boner, package, love stick, cornholer, anal impaler, baby maker, tonsil tickler, one-eyed trouser snake, anaconda, giant redwood, manhood, steamin' semen roadway, winkie, the big stick, purple-headed warrior – the list goes on. There are many words for the penis, some spoken with pride and others with contempt. Their own genitalia are of apparently infinite interest to men. They have names for them; regard women in relation to them, deciding their attractiveness based on whether they'd want to have sex with them; have rituals based around them; risk disease, divorce, dismissal, and imprisonment in order to use them; are immensely proud of them, often failing to understand why women, in the main, don't share in their cock worship; talk, brag, and joke about them; have online forums for every sort of penis (small, large, enormous, cut, uncut, potent and impotent); and have an entire social structure, that of phallocentrism, founded upon the power vested in them. It's a heady experience, having a penis.

So long as the only abuse involved is of himself, what a man does with his penis behind closed doors is taken to be his own business. What he does with it in public, however, is regulated by law. It is illegal for a man to display his penis in public if it appears to be done with the intent to cause distress and without the consent of the person to whom it is exposed. He can face a fine, prison sentence, and registration as a sex offender if caught. To the devoted flasher, unable to resist the urge to get his penis out in public, this appears to be no great deterrent.

Men who flash do so for many reasons: excitement, the naughtiness of it, the desire to feel humiliated, appreciation of what they believe to be impressive genitalia, to shock, for any reaction at all, sexual gratification, for attention, to make women smile, because it's hot and dirty, to prove themselves 'a red blooded hetero'. Some say it stems from a primitive urge, a biological imperative, a declaration of their masculinity, flaunting their genitals to impress the woman. You might say it's a sort of pre-lingual courtship ritual.

This urge, many flashers believe, is one which all men possess, but that those who don't flash are too afraid to act on. The argument that all men would flash if only they had the guts is flimsy, but it is necessary to maintain the flasher's belief that he is superior to other men because he has the bravery to do something that they do not. It is part of the same delusion that makes the flasher believe his penis is magnificent and his exposure makes him desirable to women. However much the flasher may want to believe otherwise, all men are not latent flashers. Just because they have penises doesn't mean they have any interest in or desire to gain sexual gratification from exposing them. They share the anatomy, but not the sexual proclivity. The flasher's intense preoccupation with his penis is what drives him to flash – not a primitive urge he believes to be his birthright. Men who flash are turned on by it: men who don't are not. It is a matter of taste rather than one of courage.

Though the display is public, the flashing community is an insular and private one, due to its stigma and illegality. Flashers gather in their thousands in online forums and chat rooms, some with membership in excess of 36,000, to tell tales of flashing experiences; share tips on how to flash without getting arrested; post pictures of their penises and women they want to have sex with; commiserate with and offer support to those who've been arrested, are trying to stop or have developed erectile dysfunction and so no longer enjoy flashing; brag about the size of their penises; get off on each other's stories and fantasies, boasting about how hard they came thinking about them; write reviews of a spy cam pen which enables them to film their flashes then share the women's reactions and their own ejaculations; and share links to pornographic sites such as Guess Her Muff where viewers see pictures of women clothed and try to guess what their vaginas look like, then click on the link to see the woman naked and find out if they were right. The adverts on these sites are for pills to cure erectile dysfunction and premature ejaculation, penis enhancement, dating agencies specializing in pairing up married people for affairs, and wraparound sunglasses that enable them to see if there is anyone behind them before they flash.

I told men on forums about my experiences of being flashed (once by a man sitting in his car who called me over to ask directions and was sitting there with his penis in hand and another time by a man on a motorbike who drew up beside me and lifted his shirt to show me his bared penis, both of whom I told to fuck off) and, though the general consensus was that the man on the motorbike might have been fun, had I had 'the right attitude', they decided the one in the car was self-indulgent, dishonest, and ungentlemanly. Apparently there are degrees of chivalry in flashing practices.

What flashers actually do varies from the covert to the brazen. Some push their penises through glory holes in toilet cubicle walls in the hope that they'll be sucked – a risky procedure, but one with an allegedly high rate of success. Others take pictures of their penises with their partners' friends' phones for them to find later. Masturbating in cars, known as car-jacking, provides safety and the thrill of being seen. Freeballing (going without underwear in tight clothing that shows the shape of the genitals or in loose shorts that will show them when the flasher sits down) is popular amongst those who want the pleasure of displaying but the defense, should anyone object, that they are fully clothed. Men attempting to flash covertly do so sitting in the park or launderette – anywhere public – masturbating with a newspaper on their laps; some rub their crotches against fellow commuters, blaming the crowded carriage should the woman object; others engineer situations so their partners' friends will see their penis – pulling a t-shirt up over their heads while wearing no underwear as though just getting dressed, watching the woman's reaction through the collar is a popular ploy. Others, less concerned with getting caught, will push their penises through their flies then walk around public places pretending not to realize they're on display; go into women's clothes shops and flash the staff while trying on dresses, feigning embarrassment then masturbating in the changing rooms with the thrill of their latest flash; some pretend to be urinating in alleys, waiting for an attractive woman (it must always be a woman the flasher finds attractive) to pass then flashing her.

The families of male flashers feature often in flashers' fantasies and experiences. Some simply fantasize about flashing family members, or giving brothers and fathers blowjobs; others go further and expose themselves to siblings and parents while pretending to be asleep; they text pictures of their hard-ons to their mothers, pretending it was an accident and intended for someone else; they're turned on by daughters and step-daughters, boasting of their physical attributes to other men on forums. A few have sexual relationships with their fathers, some no more than a frisson they believe exists between them, admiring their father's penis, or an occasional flash. Others involve oral and anal intercourse. Starting as teenagers, they occasionally play with or suck a father's or brother's penis while they sleep. For others, anal and oral sex with their fathers is a family ritual, begun as a child. They say they wanted it, it was spiritual, their father made them feel like a prize, and that the taboo nature of the relationship created greater excitement. Some of these relationships continue into adulthood.

Responding to stories involving family members, men in the forums want to hear more details, talk about how horny they make them, and share their own experiences. What no one points out is that these are accounts of incest, pedophilia, and ritualistic child abuse. All their fellow flashers want from the tales is sexual gratification. They respond in the same way to tales of abuse by older men and teachers: of men ejaculating onto boys' faces, rubbing their crotches against them in the classroom, and sodomizing them in their offices during detention. No one suggests they'd want to abuse children – rather, they imagine themselves in the position of the boys and report back on the load they shot thinking of the fantasy. The more graphic and extreme, the more hits, praise, and wanking the story will receive.

Female flashers posting pictures and telling of their experiences are received with equal rapture. The men demand details, they push the women to take more revealing pictures, and tell them how hard they came and how much cum they shot thinking about them. They praise the women's bodies, shaved vaginas being the most popular. Telling the women what they want to do to them, very few mention penetrative sex. There is little tenderness in their responses – the closest they get is the occasional licking of a labia or sucking of a nipple. The commonest fantasy is to ejaculate onto the woman. This, it seems, is the highest form of praise. To the flasher, no matter how appreciative he may sound in his comments, the pictures don't represent a woman or another human being. They refer to vaginas as "the goods", regarding them as a commodity like any other, and, in describing the sort of woman they find attractive, specify such things as 'waxed pussy' and 'open asshole'. To them, these women are flesh-colored objects, a life-size Jenna Jameson doll onto which they can express both their semen and their contempt.

Such attitudes towards women are not, of course, limited to flashers. Their misogyny is nothing new. What is new is the opportunity, provided by the anonymity of a chat room with an avatar and username to hide behind, to express them to an audience that not only accepts these attitudes but encourages them. In this environment, their very public actions can be revealed in private to fellow flashers, hungry for a turn-on. They can talk about getting off on watching friends having sex with their girlfriend, comatose with alcohol; boast about how turned-on they were, hearing their victim's statement read to them by the police, excited both by the account and the fact that their actions were of such significance they merited police attention; share their fantasies of being sexually humiliated or hung like Priapus; refer to looking for women at whom to flash as being on the hunt; tell of their preference for young women (though many are quick to point out that they don't flash children which may be preference or because flashing a minor carries a higher penalty); and confess to fantasizing about flashes they've done or want to do while having sex with their wives, most of whom have no idea their husbands are flashers. The desperation for sexual gratification is glaring in every post. Their lust for exposure is greater than their concern for anything else in their lives – their wives, partners, children, jobs, freedom, and homes. As a first-time offender, they are likely to receive a caution and, at most, a fine or short time in prison, but should they reoffend, they will be registered as sex offenders. For a man to risk everything for the sake of getting his penis out in public suggests more than just a penchant for a little kink. Psychiatric treatment of flashers regards it as an addiction and attempts to 'normalize' the perpetrators by a number of means, one of which is to make them watch pornographic films, the idea being that any form of sexual fantasy or practice is preferable to flashing. The massive acculturation of pornography into mainstream culture makes this treatment almost redundant: flashers are far more likely to have already absorbed attitudes and ideas from the pornography that surrounds them than to be suddenly inspired by it to stop flashing, sitting in a psychiatrist's chair.

The strictures of masculinity and the inability to meet the criteria of manliness they dictate may contribute to the flasher's urge to expose, but the creation of masculinity and the insistence on men complying with it – displaying their manliness through dominance and success in every aspect of their lives, particularly their sex lives – are done by other men. Women play no part in it. They do not create the notion of an alpha male, they subject no military subordinates to gang rape as an initiation ritual, they do not cause erectile dysfunction, they demand no swagger, yet they are punished by men who can fulfill the demands of masculinity in no way other than to display their penis, the single sure evidence of their maleness.

Yet it is neither an inability to conform to the demands

of masculinity nor his cultural environment that makes a man flash. Male flashers are entirely to blame for their actions yet it is women who assume blame for them. They worry that their breasts were too much exposed, their skirts too short, their sexuality and desire for sex were too evident – so obvious, in fact, that the flasher's sole response to them was a sexual one. He assumed that being subjected to his sexual display was what she deserved and would want. To be made to feel humiliated, shamed and anxious in order for him to get off on her response is entirely his doing, yet women blame themselves. A woman who pities a flasher, finding him ridiculous, appears to be superior to him, but really she is allowing his self-indulgence by showing no objection. Pity is a comforting response, but comfort is not what the flasher wants, nor is it what he deserves. No matter how much they may protest otherwise – say they are hoping merely for some acknowledgement and praise for their manliness – flashers know the likely response to their actions is distress and fear. There is no such thing as a harmless flash. In imposing himself upon the woman or child to whom he exposes his penis, he is committing an act of abuse from which he gains sexual satisfaction. A flash is not a harmless turn-on, a mere titillation. It is the eroticization of abuse.

To punish those who commit the crime with no more than a fine and/or prison sentence of, at most, two years and to classify the offense as minor, is to trivialize the experience of the victim and assure the flasher that his actions are of no great concern legally or socially. 15% of men who expose their penises will go on to commit further sexual offenses. Though by no means the majority, it does mean that 15 out of every 100 flashers will rape, molest, and abuse. It is clear, given the high recidivist rate, that the current practice of cautions, fines, and the possibility of a short prison sentence is hardly any great deterrent and is ineffective.

By displaying the most easily-damaged part of his body, the flasher would appear to be placing himself in a passive position. However, this is an aggressive act. It invades the space of the victim emotionally, mentally, and physically. It alters her perception of men and of sex. It forces her into a confrontation, whether she is frightened, angered, amused, or perplexed. To assume that he has a greater right to get off than she does to live her life in freedom displays arrogance and contempt. He can praise their image and masturbate over them till he's dry, but all the flasher actually feels towards women is hatred.

Female Response And Femininity

Flashing makes up 38% of all crimes, classified as minor, reported to the police by women and is, therefore, the crime that women most frequently report. However, the high recidivist rate of offenders and low rate of apprehension suggest that the police and the penal system are not the most effective channels through which to address the problem. Prior to Scottish (2009) and UK Parliament (2003) Acts, it wasn't enough for the woman to report the offense; the arresting officer had to witness it in order to arrest the offender. It is due to such unsatisfactory measures that women tend to conclude that the police as a protective male collectivity is a myth. A system that depends on a constant police presence in anticipation of flashing incidents is not reflective of civil liberties, nor is it a realistic proposition. Instead the means by which flashers were apprehended were designed to assign as little blame as possible to the offender by ensuring that, minus the credible testimony of the police officer, there would be no arrest. This procedure was based on the original intentions of the Vagrancy Act (1824) which sought to protect the reputation of innocent men from false accusations. It was thought that the stigma carried by the offense was sufficient to warrant such protective measures for men. Thus, though reports may have been investigated by the police, the pivotal power rested with the offender: if he was not apprehended by the arresting police officer, he would not face any form of reprimand for his actions. The status of the victim was assigned to be just that and no more: the woman did not deserve to be seen as a credible witness without the reinforcement of police endorsement and so remained the powerless target of an offense that would, and still does, typically go unpunished.

Subjugation to the status of 'victim', though it may be used to publicize the offense and create a bond between those affected, in no way aids the individuals themselves. In viewing herself as victimized by an exposer, the woman gives exactly the response sought by the flasher. In her attempts to ignore him, her reluctance to create a confrontation, her perception of the act as a threat directed specifically at her, caution she feels, and any changes she makes in her routine to avoid the place or situation in which she was flashed, even if she doesn't think of herself as submissive, the woman gives an exemplary display of utter submission. Such a response magnifies the villainy of the act, increasing the power of the flasher and reducing the power of the woman.

For a woman to feel like a victim, she needs to see herself as in need of protection. In viewing herself as a potential subject of attack, a woman harbors a combination of anger and fear. She would prefer to react with anger, but feels that, in all probability, she will show only fear. The anticipated and likely or actual reactions of women to flashers are testament to this fact. The anger that women carry within them could be a galvanizing force against the imposition made by such men as those who expose their genitals to them, but instead it turns inwards on the women themselves to create a self-perception of being at risk. As first-year university students we were given rape alarms during orientation week, apparently intended to give us the confidence and independence to enjoy our time at university without fear of attack because we had this thing we could use against anyone who threatened us. I carried mine in my bag everywhere I went, becoming anxious, even in daylight, if I left it in my room. Were we empowered by this device, clutched in our hands as we walked back to our dorms? No. Far from instilling confidence, we were fed a perception of ourselves as objects of attack. Had we been given self-defense lessons as well as the alarms, there might have been some amount of empowerment because we would have had skills with which to defend ourselves. As it was, we were provided with a prop, the effectiveness of which was entirely dependent on it gaining the intended response – either to frighten away the attacker or to alert a passer-by who may, or may not, have come to our aid. We were not being encouraged to be strong: we were being taught to be frightened. This is not to say that women should never feel afraid. To dismiss their desire to feel safe as weakness does not reduce their fear; it trivializes a justified and valid state of mind, but the form that these protective measures takes does not instill confidence. A woman arming herself with a rape alarm is not confident and empowered as she goes about her life: she is afraid.

A woman believing herself to be a potential object of attack has assumed a role. In looking for protection, she becomes part of a role-play in which she takes the part of a charge in need of protection and her, usually male, counterpart takes the part of protector, prepared to take on responsibility and risk for her sake. The conflict within the relationship – on an individual and social level – is in the interpretation of the roles. Does the protector offer care or oppression? Is the charge's desire for security a show of individual responsibility and autonomy or is it motivated by fear? The woman's assertion of her credibility in the reportage of exhibitionist incidents is construed as an attempt to elicit protection and show powerlessness, where it could be more constructively viewed as a declaration of her intention to combat those forces she experiences as imposing and constrictive. The authority assumed by the police officer (as representative of a predominantly male social institution) doesn't allow for or encourage such autonomy. The officer may only be doing his job, but in so doing he is operating as an integral part of mechanisms which maintain a climate of conflict between a protectionist system and the interests of those it seeks to safeguard.

The emergence of this gendered protector-charge relationship takes place during childhood. Through a process of socialization so entrenched as to be verging on social invisibility, girls are educated in the language of fear. Their actions and thoughts are informed by this social influence that, in seeking to protect them, assaults their sense of autonomy and independence. Submission when presented with displays of power becomes a naturalized response. A habit of self-doubt is absorbed, of hesitancy, confusion and acquiescence when faced with threat or confrontation. A confident girl is a willful or stubborn one, her assertiveness discouraged, where the same trait would be encouraged in a boy.

It is unclear at what point a child begins to react to flashers as an adult would. It is likely to be around the time when she begins to become aware of herself as a sexualized being, and when she, or her friends, starts to be sexually active – an age increasingly early. It is at this time that she begins to regard her body as possessing some sort of sexual value; whether she feels this to be as a passive object of desire, or as an active individual, seeking sexual satisfaction for her own pleasure. There is a clumsy shift from a self-perception that regards sexualized attention directed at her as something unfamiliar, perhaps confusing as though it were somehow misplaced, to that of a woman, aware of the sexual value of her body. This developmental stage is also the point at which she enters into the dialogue of power based on her gender. All around her she sees images of herself represented by women assuming positions of subjugation to male desire. The teen and women's magazines she reads, the billboards she passes, the lad mags on the shelves at the supermarket, and the films she watches all attest to such a position as natural, conventional, acceptable, and to be expected. It is at this point that, as well as discovering the penis as a sexual object (rather than merely a reproductive one) she first becomes aware of the power associated with it and the responses expected to it. Though they may also associate them with pleasure, the blurring of biology, sex, and power in the minds of women instils within them an inherent fear of the use of male genitals for insult or threat.

Women's fear of flashing is founded on the fact that they are uncertain how far men will take their attempts to dominate them. The most common concern expressed by women is that they are afraid the exposure will progress to assault, rape or murder: hence the avoidance of confrontation. A man with nothing but his penis to hand is exposing the most easily damaged part of his body, yet he is perceived as a threat and his actions as aggressive. Taking the definition of violent acts to be those resulting in long-term or permanent damage to the victim's ability to function, flashing is a form of violence. In view of the alterations made in the behavior of many of the women who have been flashed at, it is apparent that, for many women, both "long-term" and "permanent" impairment had been inflicted. He may claim otherwise, but this is how the flasher wants his actions to be perceived – even if he doesn't intend to touch the woman, being seen as a threat and showing his penis to the woman against her will is part of the thrill.

The sleight of hand in this conjuring act is the deft internalization in a woman of herself as vulnerable to attack.

What is suggested by the woman's assumption of guilt for the exposer's actions is a feeling of shame at her own sexual potency. It is as though her assertion of sexual autonomy is an unnatural and ultimately undesirable expression of independence that should be confined. As he exposes his genitals, the flasher acknowledges her sexual value as he attempts to debase it. If she feels shamed or guilty, it is because she believes his view of her as a sexual being is more significant than her own.

But women are not only afraid. Ask them about their experiences of being flashed, or how they think they would respond if they were, and rather than being angry, resentful, defensive they are aggressive, amused, shaken, aghast, violated, shocked, embarrassed, dirtied, threatened, disturbed, humiliated, disgusted, indignant, intimidated, pissed-off, repulsed, put-upon, and unimpressed. This range of responses suggests the possibility of radical change in the way in which women regard and respond to male flashers. Fear and submission need not be the only reaction. If she can perceive a man's exposure of his penis as a trivial – even laughable – act, its awesome nature is lost. Though she may believe otherwise, flashing is not, in and of itself, dangerous. The penis does not intimidate. It is the threat associated with it, yet in brandishing nothing more than this fleshly appendage, the man could hardly be more vulnerable.

For women to change the way they regard the flasher, it isn't enough just to acknowledge that. We need to make fundamental changes. We can do little about masculinity: men have manufactured it, choosing the aspects of what the phallus, as symbol of male power, represents and used them to best serve their own interests. It is hard enough to effect change in one man, let alone in a transnational social construct. Male violence will never be eradicated either on the mass scale of warfare or in the home. However, that doesn't mean we can do nothing to fight it: we can still campaign for those who commit crimes against women to be brought to justice and give voice to women sold, abused, and silenced by oppression and fear.

And we can change femininity. We can change the way in which we regard and treat ourselves, our sexuality, our bodies, and our right to be free. These should be defined by no one but ourselves. We are bombarded with images, attitudes, and opinions, all telling us how we should perceive our own selves, most frequently our bodies. Women's bodies are sold and used to sell: they are a commodity, their ownership colonized by those who decide how much they are worth, from the pimp to the plastic surgeon. We have come to regard ourselves as vessels for these attitudes, assimilating them to the point where they become our reality. We absorb too much, we take into ourselves the perception of how we should be: our homes sterile, our bodies thin and hairless, our sexual desires those of the porn star, borne with the same vacant smile. We starve and mutilate our bodies; we cower, taking up as little space as possible. We know we shouldn't cross our legs so the man beside us, thighs splayed, can take up two thirds of the seat, but we do it anyway. We have as much right as any man to occupy the space around us, to be free in it, yet we let the threat of attack limit our movements. The imposition of the flasher into our space should make us furious, but instead we take on his hatred and blame ourselves for the attack. Instead of saying how dare he, we wonder what we might have done to provoke him and feel sullied, frightened, and ashamed. We already have so much in our lives that is negative: we worry we won't be able to feed our children, we castigate ourselves for eating at all, our bodies are ravaged by a desperate wish for agelessness and by the exhaustion of bearing children we can only hope to care for, and our minds are consumed by the misogyny that surrounds us. We do not need to add to these concerns the fear created by the flasher. Femininity does not need to tie in with the traits of masculinity – we do not need to be weak to complement his assertiveness or frightened because he may be aggressive. Femininity exists entirely separately to masculinity. We should be defining it, not allowing men and misogyny to do it for us – they provide no model on which to build a multifarious self. The way we view our bodies, our sexuality, and ourselves, and the way we want to live and be are ours to determine. Ours should be an autonomous self not a victimized one. The flasher should not distress us: confronted with him we should be reminded of our will to defy.

Mapping Masculinity: The Psychiatrist's Perspective

As far as the psychiatric profession is concerned, the purpose of treatment is to rid the flasher of his abnormal behavior and replace it with sexual tastes and activities that are more in keeping with the behavior of a man of normal urges. It's a flawed approach, based as it is on a subjective view of what constitutes normality and abnormality, but a belief in the existence of a normalized male underlies all forms of treatment and opinions on the activity.

As a group male flashers tend to be characterized by the psychiatric profession as 'timid, unassertive individuals who were lacking in social skills and had difficulty recognizing and handling aggression and hostility'.[1] Analysis of their sexual relationships reveals that although 'relatively few have other overt psychological disturbances...in those who marry, marital adjustment is poorer than average'.[2] Generalized statements such as 'unsure of themselves sexually, they are usually immature and undemanding in their gender role' are frequently made, and remain largely undisputed.[3] The typical flasher is socially inept and perceives himself as unmanned by his inability to conform to the criteria of masculinity presented to him by the culture that surrounds him. Typically, he is 'a quiet, submissive, "nice guy" with well-developed feelings of inadequacy, inferiority and insecurity in interpersonal and social relations' which he attempts to counter by seeking the 'feelings of strength and manhood likely to result from exhibiting himself in a fully erect state'.[4] Even for those who expose a flaccid penis, their actions tend to be fueled by this desire to exert a sense of manliness through flashing: they may be unable or unwilling to exemplify dominant notions of masculinity, but they can assert their maleness by displaying the anatomical proof.

Theories as to the causes of flashing are diverse and generally inconclusive. There are, however, some recurring themes in the explanations offered by flashers themselves. One such theme is a professed contempt for women. Statements such as 'when it's happening I'm not conscious of anything except this feeling of being contemptuous toward particular women and wanting to give one a shock' recur in interviews and case studies. The factors that account for such an attitude towards women are said to be based on the social process of gender role construction. There is an inherent ambivalence embedded in men towards women that is fueled by women's growing autonomy. The simultaneous devaluation of citadels of male power has created a shift in gender dynamics that has not been accompanied by compensatory alterations in the markers of masculinity. Thus the structures on which male autocracy is based are undermined, causing an eruption of anxiety that is not countered by alternative modes for the assertion of strength. Sexual autonomy or independence shown by women batters male insecurity. As a result, to mask the insecurity this creates, men who feel affected by it are more likely to react to any challenge by lashing out. It is a common feature that men become almost amnesiac about violent incidents, as if to admit or recognize them is to see their tenuous security undermined even further. To admit that all they have is physical power is, in any useful way, a confession of absolute weakness. Many studies report an exclusion of all conscious rationalization in favor of an indefinable sense of gratification that is frequently accompanied by guilt or shame following the exposure. The flasher can't or won't determine the cause of his actions on any conscious level.

It has been suggested that sexual practices termed 'perversions' – as flashing is – are instigated by the desire to manage and maintain self-esteem at a level which provides the individual with sufficient confidence to function socially to some degree.[5] Unable to satisfy the criteria of social functionality in their entirety, the individual enters into a context in which the parameters can be controlled by self-constructed criteria. He can achieve some level of self-satisfaction by meeting the standards set within the insular environment in which he measures success. In the case of the flasher, the reaction of the female spectator provides the reinforcement necessary to improve his self-esteem. The flasher may not feel able to meet the demands of his gender, but by displaying his genitals he is at least asserting his maleness. This is, of course, a tenuously structured process and is entirely dependent on the spectator demonstrating the desired reaction. No matter how great or sustaining his belief that he has impressive genitals, though women may be shocked, they are seldom impressed by the flasher's display. They do not believe it to be magnificent as he would wish or imagines it to be. However, the shock, embarrassment, fear, and anger with which the woman may respond assure the flasher that his genitals are impressive enough to warrant a substantial reaction. This would also help explain the general lack of precautions taken by flashers to avoid the police: arrest further acknowledges the magnificence of his genitals.

A number of proponents of behavioral analysis of flashing view the activity as the result of a conditioning process, somehow instigated by a deviant sexual encounter. The genesis of the activity is in a 'crucial, although possibly accidental, sexual experience' which later becomes the subject of masturbatory fantasy.[6] It's argued that the commitment of this experience to fantasy heightens its erotic appeal: 'it is in accordance with conditioning theory that any stimulus which regularly precedes ejaculation by the correct time interval should become more and more sexually exciting'.[7] Only those sexual experiences perceived to be pleasurable become incorporated into fantasy, which offers some explanation as to why not all individuals who have deviant sexual encounters later experience them as erotic in fantasy form. In the case of the flasher, accidental exposure can be given enough erotic appeal to become part of his sexual fantasies, increasing the excitement it causes, driving him to replicate it in reality. It is assumed that by educating the individual in 'normal' sexual stimuli, the deviant fantasies will be removed and lose their erotic appeal.

Rather than locate a cathartic experience as the origin of sexual deviance, other theorists believe it stems from the individual's upbringing, their argument based on the assumption that parents may be responsible for intentionally or unintentionally normalizing certain sexual practices which are disapproved of socially. Although there is virtually no data with which to support this view, it is possible that the prevalence of sexual 'abnormality' within the parental relationship could provide the child with an association between the practices and parental approval. It is widely accepted that, as the most prominent site of social conditioning and adjustment, the home is also the arbiter of normality. The longevity and context of exposure to so-called deviant sexual practices may result in the individual receiving greater arousal from 'abnormal' sexual stimulus, than from 'normal' stimulus. Behavioral therapy is designed to redress this balance by removing the arousal caused by the deviant stimulus and replacing it with one that is approved of socially, such as pornography.

It's not a new area of psychiatric concern, but there is yet to be a definitive, conclusive study or treatment proven to be successful in the long-term. The majority of flashers who undergo psychiatric treatment do so while in prison or as a condition of their release. As a result, most clinical studies are based on those convicted for the crime and, therefore, limited in scope to a group pre-selected by the penal system. How effective the treatments would be on men who had no interest in giving up flashing or hadn't been ordered to undergo treatment is difficult to say. If the urge is as all-consuming as flashers claim, it's likely treatment wouldn't diminish it in the least. That said, given the invasive nature of most forms of treatment, it's possible even the most devoted flasher would feel some effect.

In order to transform the flasher into the embodiment of a well-adjusted man, the tools used most frequently are punishment and humiliation. They're not called that, of course – rather, they're known as such things as the Sexual Orientation Method, covert sensitization, and aversion therapy – but to punish and humiliate the flasher into giving up his deviant ways is the basis of all forms of treatment.

Though most flashers treated are adults, treatment is occasionally provided for children, with the intention of normalizing their sexual activities and tastes before they reach adulthood. In once such case, under the supervision of psychiatrists MacCulloch, Williams, and Birtles, a twelve-year-old adolescent who fantasized about and flashed older women was encouraged to find a more 'age-appropriate heterosexual object choice' through the use of electro-shock therapy. Using a treatment known as the Sexual Orientation Method,[8] the adolescent was first shown slides of mature women and adolescent girls in random sequence. Failure to remove the slides of mature women within eight seconds resulted in an electric shock, whereas he could look at the girls for as long as he liked without punishment. He was later shown slides of women only until his response to them was reported as indifference or even dislike and he removed the slide within 1 to 2 seconds. The slides of the adolescent girls were then displayed, along with the older women. The adolescent was allowed to ask to see the pictures of the girls, though his request was met with random acquiescence by the supervisor, with the intention of conditioning him to realize that his desire for women would not always be reciprocated. The treatment had two aims: an avoidance of and aversion to older women, and an attraction to female adolescents. The results indicated success: the adolescent reported the absence of the urge to flash, lessening anxiety regarding heterosexual relationships, and masturbatory fantasy that was limited to adolescent girls and did not contain any flashing.[9] From these results, the psychiatrists, no doubt, congratulated one another on the successful treatment, but telling a twelve-year-old boy how he should view sex and sexuality at so young an age, teaching him to expect rejection by women, and punishing him if he fantasizes about anything other than adolescent girls hardly sounds like the basis for normal sexual development, by any definition.

An alternative form of aversion-based therapy, known as covert sensitization, is commonly used with sex offenders. This procedure aims to create an association between flashing and an unpleasant experience. Barry Maletzky provided one of the first reports of its use with flashers, using valeric acid to induce nausea. Maletzky and the patient devised a fantasy scenario based on the patient's imagination and on past experience of flashing which was recounted during the session. As the patient's sexual excitement increased, Maletzky would introduce suggestions of such unpleasant experiences as nausea, vomiting, and pain into the scenario, and hold an open bottle of valeric acid under the patient's nose. As the scenario progressed, the patient imagined leaving the scene, the acid was removed, and he was encouraged to relax. In follow-up sessions the patient's fantasies were monitored, along with any flashing incidents or urge to do so. The final validation of treatment success was measured using a 'temptation test'. This was designed to tempt the flasher to expose himself by presenting him with a woman hired by the therapist. The situation and appearance of the woman were tailored to his previous fantasies and experience and were presented at the end of treatment and after one year. Of the ten exhibitionists treated in this way by Maletzky, nine passed their temptation tests. In addition, most of the subjects reported 'improved heterosexual adjustment and job performance', as well as 'more self confidence and pride once they were free of urges to expose themselves'.[10]

These treatments seek to alter the private associations of the individual with imagined exhibitionist acts; other methods are intended to do the opposite, removing any control the flasher has over the situation. One such treatment is designed to provoke anxiety in the patient by making him undress in front of a mixed-sex audience.[11] While he undresses he describes flashing experiences to the audience and is filmed for later analysis. The patient is unable to dictate any of the conditions under which he undresses, including the distance between him and the audience (this is generally set at around 4-5 feet, presumed to be considerably less than the comfortable distance set by the average flasher, though tastes and practices vary).

During the exposure to the audience the most common emotions felt by the flasher are anxiety and tension. For many 'sweating is usually so profuse that it runs from the axillae to the legs irrespective of the ambient temperature' during the experience.[12] Many then feel shame, disgust, embarrassment, and, occasionally, anger watching the film. It is assumed by those supervising the treatment that the extreme level of stress presses the patient to question habitually assumed attitudes towards his behavior and the response of others. There is also the intention that the negative association of anxiety with flashing will help to fight the urge to flash or stop it altogether – the flasher's abnormal urges will be replaced with ones more in keeping with those of a normal man.

In a similar treatment, the patient was made to flash female psychiatric nurses in a waiting room.[13] In the case reported, the patient was instructed to approximate as closely as possible his actions in public, while the nurses were to respond with indifference and leave after fifteen minutes. In later sessions the nurses made eye contact with the patient, staring at him while he attempted to flash them. This reaction caused the man to feel unable to continue touching his genitals and to lose his erection. Though such a procedure did not provide direct punishment for flashing, it removed the reinforcement generally provided by the response of the witness to the act in public. Any punishment was thought to be derived from feelings of guilt and shame on the part of the patient, along with the confrontation induced by the eye contact made by the nurses. No one seems to have carried out a follow-up study of the nurses to find out what they thought about the experience or if it affected, in any way, their attitudes towards flashers.

Another approach uses aversion therapy to make the

flasher associate flashing with anxiety, then offers him alternative sources of arousal that are considered acceptable. Practitioners of this technique maintain that the incorporation of flashing experiences into fantasy strengthens their erotic appeal and so treatment procedures seek to replace these deviant fantasies with ones deemed normal.[14] Fantasies centering on sex with either the wife/girlfriend or women in pornography are constructed. Though the flasher's fantasies are considered perverse, deviant, and abnormal, replacing them with pornography – material that has been judged misogynist or, at the very least, insensitive to the desires of women – is apparently preferable. Pornography has become socially sanctioned to such a degree that it is prescribed in psychiatric treatment. The desired outcome of this procedure is the removal of flashing from fantasy and reality, accompanied by their replacement with heterosexual fantasy and practice. This construction of appropriate masculine behavior is founded on a tenuous structure designed to sacrifice alternative sexual practice for the mediocrity of dubious adjustment. The measure of the success of this process is based on a system of surveillance that monitors and, where it is deemed necessary, intervenes in the sexual relationships of the treated patient. 'Whenever appropriate, wives are included in initial discussions prior to treatment, frequent sexual intercourse is encouraged, and concern about sexual relationships is monitored and discussed during treatment'.[15] Such a procedure is one which removes sex from a pleasurable and bodily context and places it under clinical scrutiny. It's questionable the extent to which this is likely to encourage 'normal' sexual relations in even the most well-adjusted individual.

Various forms of drug therapy may also be provided, either alone or, more commonly, in conjunction with behavior-based treatments. While they might not stop the flasher wanting to flash or doing so, treatments such as anti-androgen therapy and the use of drugs like Thioridazine cause temporary impotence, inability to ejaculate, and reduction of sex drive.[16] Because male virility is assumed, in this approach, to be the impetus behind the desire to expose, its removal provides a period in which the flasher lacks the necessary motivation or ability to flash (unless he is happy to expose a flaccid penis) and may, therefore, be both more receptive to behavioral therapy and less likely to expose.

Where behavioral and drug therapies are deemed ineffective, those involved in treatment may resort to surgery. Though rare, there have been cases of the use of castration on apparently inexorable flashers.

As far as the majority of psychiatric, psychoanalytic, and sociological studies are concerned, flashing is an exclusively male activity. Legally it can be committed by a woman, but there are few reported cases. Women make up only 0.3% of all convicted sex offenders; of this number, the minority are for flashing.[17] Where a woman does expose her body in public and is arrested, she will be subject to the same prosecution procedures as a man, but her actions will probably be interpreted differently by those to whom she exposes herself and those treating her, largely because she is not seen to pose any threat.

Due to the infrequency with which it is reported, there are few case studies of female flashers, but those that have been recorded offer some insight into the difference in meaning ascribed to male and female flashing. One of the most in-depth investigations carried out was by psychiatrist Charles Grob in 1985, who, in attempting to treat a woman, dubbed "M", who displayed her breasts and genitals, made a number of observations that are reflective of the view of female flashing generally adopted by the psychiatric sector.[18] M suffered a childhood of neglect and abuse in foster homes, an orphanage and with her father, whom she believed to have incestuous designs on her. She later married, had two children, attempted suicide, was divorced from her husband, and embarked on a career in which she excelled. In the midst of a depressive and anxious state following dismissal from her job and the loss of custody of her children, she began to flash. At first she sunbathed naked, feeling excited and aroused when low-flying aircraft circled over her; then she began to drive onto the motorway to expose her breasts and genitals to truck drivers. Not wishing to have any actual contact with the drivers, she would allow them to pursue her for as long as 30 minutes before exiting the motorway. On average she drove as far as 600 miles each weekend in order to expose herself to drivers, saying she did so for both sexual and emotional reasons. Turned on by the attention and finding in it some sense of self-worth, she compulsively craved it. Grob concluded his study with the verdict that the woman was 'an intensely narcissistic individual who was virtually addicted to attention-seeking in order to establish and sustain a sense of self-esteem'.[19] His findings led him to believe that she 'sought to frustrate and control her male audience by her particular method of exhibitionism, perhaps as an outlet for her anger, envy, and frustrated identification with men'.[20] With quite astoundingly archaic reasoning, Grob assigned to the woman 'a partial masculine identity [which] may be attributed to this woman who had achieved notable success in a previously male-dominated field', and ruled that her 'breast and genital exhibitionism became the symbolic and primitive expression of this need [for attention] when a more socially acceptable form of exhibitionism (her job) was lost'.[21]

Thus, the assumption by a woman of supposedly masculine characteristics is offered as the only viable explanation for actions that are usually only carried out by men - that and her 'intensely narcissistic' personality that led her to seek attention through the display of her body.

Fellow psychiatrist, Art O'Connor, carried out a similar study of female sex offenders, a number of whom were flashers. His findings echoed those of Grob in declaring that the women all exposed out of their need for attention. O'Connor's report provided some variance in saying that sexual gratification appeared to be absent from the motivations of the women.[22] It's a conclusion with which the women displaying their vaginas and breasts and telling their tales in forums and chat rooms would disagree, highlighting the frequent distance between research and reality.

While male flashers are, in the main, said not to manifest overtly abnormal psychology, in the medical arena, female flashing tends to be associated with such factors as drug and alcohol abuse, psychiatric disorders (hypomania and depression, for example), childhood sexual abuse, and parental neglect. Where it is a compulsion driven by such tremendous damage to the individual, it is an act fueled by weakness. In contrast to the motives of the majority of male flashers, his exertion of power is her loss of control.

This is the medicalization of flashing: men deconstructed and clumsily put back together so their behavior, attitudes, and sexual proclivities are better suited to those expected of their sex. It is an attempt to dissect both the man and masculinity, to draw out the traits of that cultural icon, the phallic male. Confident, successful, manly, and commanding, he is the ultimate alpha male – a creature worthy of the precepts of phallocentrism that posit him as an unimpeachable authority. This is the man the flasher is supposed to be, but is incapable of doing so, so he expresses his masculinity through exposing his penis, the incontrovertible proof of his maleness. It is, ultimately, a display of weakness in which the flasher presents himself as a passive object, quite in contrast to the dynamic that ought to exist between a man and a woman. The man should be dominant and the woman submissive. We are used to seeing women as objects and as passive displays – that is not the position in which men should be placed. To have the roles reversed threatens the conventional dynamic and must be prevented with any means necessary: valeric acid, pornography, electro-shock therapy, humiliation, and the policing of sexual relation-ships and fantasies. The flasher is not an autonomous individual – he is a victim of the culture that surrounds him, of his upbringing, of women's growing power in arenas that were previously, if not exclusively male, then male-dominated. He is an image of failed manhood and must be rehabilitated into a fully functioning, well-adjusted example of his sex. This is the psychodynamic take on flashing.

It's an interesting perspective and one which, on paper, makes a great deal of sense. People under pressure to conform will find ways of subverting their situation. It's why we get piercings, run off with people our parents don't approve of, dye our hair scarlet and declare ourselves anarchists, leave spouses and children to travel the world, take up rubber fetishism, or shatter the glass ceiling and move on to CEO. The flasher's response to this pressure is to take out his penis in public – he might not be able to meet the criteria required of his gender, but that doesn't make him any less of a man and dammit he's got the anatomy to prove it. But it isn't enough just to blame it on the social process of gender role construction. Nor is it enough to blame it on women and their increasing power. Men flashed long before women had even basic human rights – it wasn't a practice taken up concurrent with the rise of feminism. Women already assume blame where they should not. This ought not to be given medical approval as though both individual women and our sex at large were responsible for the flasher's actions. Though upbringing does, of course, affect people in later life, blaming the flasher's sexual proclivities entirely on the parents scapegoats them and infantilizes him. Though the treatments are invasive – physically, emotionally, and mentally – the flasher, as a man, remains curiously untouched. The assumption is that culture, women, and upbringing are to blame rather than the man himself. This thinking permits psychiatrists to prescribe pornography and indoctrinate a child into believing that the only sexual fantasies acceptable are about adolescent girls. Conspicuously absent is the suggestion that the flasher is responsible for his actions. If making a man of him is the intention, chasing that specter of the normalized male, surely insisting he take responsibility for his actions, acting in full autonomy, would be more beneficial than telling him it's not his fault and here are some women faking it just for him to masturbate over. Deviant, perverted, abnormal, aberrant – call it what you will – the flasher chooses to do it. The simple truth about flashing is not that it is a symptom of anything. Women don't make them do it, nor do their parents or culture. Men flash because they get off on it. It's an urge they want to follow so they do.

Flashing and the Law

One of the earliest bureaucratic social encounters with flashing was in 16th century Italy where men could seek to formally dispel rumors of impotence that could be used as grounds for the annulment of marriage by exhibiting their erect penis to priests, jurists, and physicians and, occasionally, demonstrating ejaculation. The practice continued into 17th and 18th century France, but then seemed to fade from usage. Much to the relief of the men subjected to it, no doubt. Such a procedure may have met with acceptance for legal and religious purposes, but in public, exposure of the genitals was regarded as a mark of social inferiority. Guides to demeanor served the reader with such dictums as that of Richard Weste in his publication, The Book of Demeanor and the Allowance and Disallowance of Certaine Misdemeanors in Companie:

Let not thy privy members be
layd open to be view'd
it is so shameful and abhorred,
detestable and rude.[23]

Though the male fashion at times called for the exhibition of genital attributes under cover of such articles as the cod-piece that drew attention to and exaggerated the size of the penis, actual exposure of the genitals was not an accepted part of social display. However, in some cultural climates, as late as the 19th century, flashing was regarded as a natural component of courtship: in order to prove his virility, the man would display his (presumably erect) penis to the woman as part of the seduction. Not exactly subtle, but I suppose it enabled the woman to take penis size into consideration when trying to decide whether or not to marry the man presenting himself to her.

An alternative take on flashing as a courtship ritual was that the man exposed his penis to the woman in order to effect an ersatz defloration: the shock and embarrassment of the woman provided some similitude of what he might hope for or expect from sex with her, enough to satisfy, however briefly, his inept sexual advances and clumsy attempts to woo her.

There are also reports on the Bolton Races in England during the 1860s at which arrests were made for indecency. The races were run by men and boys either naked or scantily clad, for the entertainment of a predominantly male audience: a curious example of male nudity set up as a spectacle for other men.

It appears that the shame and inappropriateness associated with flashing originated, in Britain, with a social elite who came to view it as a sign of either mental instability or working class immorality. Hence the inclusion of indecent exposure in the legislation that criminalized such acts as attempts to procure alms, unlicensed prostitution and peddling, homelessness, carrying burglary tools, fortune-telling and palmistry, and the abandonment of wives and children. Not that the upper classes were above such antics.

In the late 18th century the issues surrounding bodily exposure became indentured to the system of social divisions: the extent to which shame on the part of the exposer and observer was felt was determined by social status. Though a man might feel disgrace at having his body exposed to equals or superiors, being seen by inferiors was not a matter for great concern. Such a view remained prevalent into the Victorian era when it was amplified by an emergent abhorrence of male nudity. The censoring of male genitals reached such extremes that genitalia were removed from statues and concealed in paintings. It was at this time that the medico-legal alliance surfaced, apparently spurred by the increasing number of cases of male exhibitionism. Flashing was now both a legal and medical concern, though it was not until the late 1800s, when French psychiatrist Ernest-Charles Lasegue coined the term 'exhibitionist', that it became a recognized psychiatric syndrome.[24]

Prior to the passage of the Vagrancy Act (1824) acts of indecent exposure were punishable under ecclesiastical ruling. Though the ecclesiastic court of the Star Chamber lost the power to inflict capital punishment and to judge matters of religious nonconformity in 1677, the common law court of the King's Bench assumed the role of custos morum at this time and continued to prosecute offenses deemed to be counter to Christianity. It maintained the principles that the Star Chamber had applied to cases of indecent exposure - along with blasphemy and ribaldry - in judging them to be profane acts rather than legal misdemeanors. This arrangement was based on the entanglement of Church and State in a reciprocal relationship of enforcement: the Christian establishment supported the State and its law with the assumption that statute would reflect ecclesiastical interests. This principle was gradually undermined, but it was not until 1824 that an offense that had been viewed as a profanity was transferred to secular legal control.

On 21 June 1824 Royal Assent was given for the passage of the Vagrancy Act (1824),[25] a parliamentary decision that for the first time defined the offense of indecent exposure under legal statute. The Act set out three categories of vagrant liable to face prosecution: the idle and disorderly, the vagrant, and the incorrigible rogue. It was the latter category which was to be dealt with under section 4 of the Act, declaring that 'every person willfully, openly, lewdly and obscenely exposing his person with intent to insult any female...shall be deemed a rogue and vagabond' and punished accordingly.[26]

Punishment of those convicted under the vagrancy legislation had formerly included whipping, boring the ears, slitting the nose, and branding the forehead, but this was deemed not only excessive for those prosecuted for indecent exposure, but also likely to encourage the individual to seek sympathy and to recommit. It was replaced under the 1824 Act with fine and imprisonment, a decision based on the assumption that the damage to the reputation of the exposer legally consigned to infamy as a 'rogue and vagabond' was sufficient deterrent against recidivistic offenses.

The arresting police officer had to witness the offense, a stipulation intended to protect innocent men from false accusations, and it had to have been carried out in public.

Any person who 'willfully and indecently exposes his person', along with anyone caught committing such heinous crimes as ringing doorbells, flying kites, beating a carpet before 8 am (though doormats were exempt), having a pigsty too close to the street, or obstructing traffic while shoeing a horse, could also be prosecuted under the Town Police Clauses Act (1847).[27]

The Army Act (1881) declared it an offense for a person 'subject to military law to commit any disgraceful conduct of an indecent kind'.[28]

Definitions, stipulations, and forms of punishment shifted as the crime was included in further Acts, amended by the Criminal Justice Act (1925)[29] and later contained within the Public Order Act (1986).[30] However, the basic objection to the offense remained: it was an outrage to public decency.

Once apprehended, the offender had to have been seen to have committed such an act as to outrage public decency, given to mean a gross transgression of common propriety of significant offense to the average person and judged to be of 'a lewd, obscene or disgusting character'.[31]

As appropriate, such a classification was intended to shift in accordance with social mores. However, as the outcome of Regina v Lunderbech (1991) attested to, proof of outrage was not necessary: it need only be shown that the act was of appropriate character as to have potentially caused outrage.[32]

A stipulation that remained throughout all Acts was that the offense be carried out in public. This classification was of equally dubious grounding, and subject to numerous qualifications and anomalies. The original ruling in statute was that the act of exposure must have been observed by at least one person in order that it be judged to have occurred in public (Regina v Farrell (1862)[33] and Regina v Mayling (1963)).[34] This, however, was over-ruled in a number of cases in favor of more encompassing definitions of what constituted the term 'public'. It could be ruled that the exposure was carried out in public where the statement of one witness, plus evidence that others could have seen was given (Knuller v DPP (1972));[35] where the general public did not have access, but could poten-tially go (Regina v Wellard (1884));[36] in private - generally reserved for cases involving exposure to minors (Regina v Walker (1996));[37] where the exposure was recorded on security camera; or where the police witnessed the act and were regarded as representative of the public and its opinion.

Where sufficient criteria were met, the offense was deemed indictable at common law, and could be subject to both fine and imprisonment. It was most commonly dealt with using the Vagrancy Act (1824), under which, if convicted, the exposer may have been subject to three months' imprisonment or a fine not exceeding level three; or, if on a repeat offense and committal to the Crown Court for sentence, one year's imprisonment. Most notably in cases of recidivist offenses, psychiatric treatment was frequently a further stipulation at conviction. Although the original law was concerned solely with male offenders, under later legislation the act may have been carried out by a male or female person. There are few reported cases of female exposers (Regina v Elliot and White (1861)[38] is a rare exception and the prosecution was for intercourse in a public place), but where they do occur they are subject to the same prosecution procedures as male offenders.

Although an individual could, in theory, still be charged under the Vagrancy, Town Police Clauses, Army, and Public Order Acts, it is more likely to be done so under the Sexual Offences Act (2003)[39] and Sexual Offences (Scotland) Act (2009).[40]

There is no stipulation in these Acts that the offense be carried out in public. Nor is it required that the arresting officer witness it. The focus is on consent of the victim and the intent of the perpetrator. They are designed to protect the public from the male flasher, but their stipulations could be seen as attempts to protect the female flasher rather than those at whom she flashes.

Under Scottish law, a person may be charged with 'sexual exposure' if he or she intentionally exposes his or her genitals in a sexual manner for the purposes of 'obtaining sexual gratification, humiliating, distressing or alarming' without the victim consenting and without any reasonable belief that he or she consents.[41]

Under UK Parliament law, there is no direct reference to

consent or sexual gratification. A person will be found guilty of exposure and may be subject to fine and imprisonment for up to two years, if 'he intentionally exposes his genitals and he intends that someone will see them and be caused alarm or distress'.[42] The use of 'he' is taken to mean persons either male or female as both may be prosecuted for exposure.

The removal of the stipulation that the offense must be carried out in public was done, largely in response to naturists' concerns that, by being naked, they may be charged with indecent exposure. Under the assumption that there is no sexual gratification sought from their actions, streakers are also exempt and regarded, at most, as a public nuisance.

For all the legal attention that has been given to flashing, it seems there is no deterrent great enough to stop people who want to flash from doing so. Even counting only those who join forums and chat rooms, flashing is a fairly popular pastime with tens of thousands taking part. The number of participants appears to be increasing, despite penalties that could cost them everything. It could be that flashers are unconcerned about the risk of prosecution. Though they may face the death penalty, people still murder – every crime is committed in spite of its consequences so there is no reason to expect flashing to be any exception.

No longer fashionable as a courtship ritual (not that I've encountered, anyway, though I suppose it's possible the men in the car and on the motorbike were attempting, bewilderingly, to woo me), flashing has been medicalized and criminalized. The thinking behind the criminalization of the act is fairly straightforward and the protection the measures seek to provide necessary. What is tremendously more complex is their other purpose: the policing of human desire. Whether through medical monitoring of fantasy or criminal prosecution, this is impossible. As long as flashers feel the urge to flash and gain sexual gratification from doing so, nothing will stop them.

Conclusion: The Demise of the Good Old-Fashioned Roll in the Hay

Sexuality is, to put it mildly, a convoluted subject. From a process of reproduction, sex has become something of labyrinthine complexity. It is far more than just our sex organs. Whether we're aware of it or want to, we bring to sex our pasts, desires, preconceptions, prejudices, morals, insecurities, and emotions. There are expectations of both men and women – everyone wants to be thought of as good in bed, but what that involves has become increasingly demanding. We're all to be porn stars. Girls as young as eleven are pressured by their peers (their female friends as much as the boys) into replicating the sex their boyfriends have seen in porn. Admit you like the missionary position and you might as well declare yourself a Puritan and get thee to a nunnery. No, we're all supposed to be as limber as a Cirque du Soleil contortionist. Sex isn't just a fun way to spend the afternoon, it's a competition. We try to be better than the last lover – or, indeed, anyone the other person has ever had sex with. Sex is to be mind-blowing, ne'er before known heights of ecstasy, unforgettable and impossible to surpass. We count our orgasms, rating our lovers by the number of times they make us come in a night. Even if we wouldn't want to venture into the world of slings and hardcore S&M, we're blasé about the more extreme sexual practices because that's the fashionable way to be. We buy into the highly lucrative concept that our sex lives need to be spiced up – thrilling at all times. At the mellow end of the market are scented candles and a romantic dinner; role play and dressing up usually make the list; then there's a little light bondage of the Ann Summers handcuffs and whipped cream variety; and sex manuals are a must, though nothing of the boring old Joy of Sex sort – they have to be fun fun fun. On and on it goes in the quest for the perfect shag.

No matter how modern all this might make us feel, there remains the double standard between men and women regarding sexual mores. There are no derogatory words for a promiscuous man, but innumerable ones for a woman. How many men a woman has sex with and how soon after meeting shouldn't be worth even mentioning, but it is the subject of countless and constant debates. Living by the rules or by one's own ought to be a given, but women frequently lie about the number of lovers they've had and the extent of their experience, downplaying both to their partners. Porn encourages us to act like a slut in the bedroom, but apparently we're not supposed to actually be one out of it. I don't think anyone quite knows why we do this, why we have such contrasting views of male and female behavior, but it's a practice that every generation adopts, to a greater or lesser extent, and has done so over centuries.

I'm not arguing in favor of mediocre sex. No one wants that. I don't think men should, à la Christian missionaries, pray for god's forgiveness for taking carnal pleasure and their wives' bodies be concealed by full-length white night-dresses with a hole embroidered in the shape of a cross over their vaginas. Sex is supposed to be fun. It's supposed to be about people – real life ones, not the ones pornography, magazines, adverts, and billboards tell us we should be. The anal sex her boyfriend saw onscreen shouldn't be a part of an 11-year-old girl's life. Her life should be about her – what she wants to do and what she enjoys – not what porn told her boyfriend she ought to be. You'd think we'd grow out of that, but the idea that sex is a performance to impress our lover surrounds us and, inevitably, affects the way we view ourselves and those with whom we have sex. In attempting to emulate the moves of a porn star, women are understudying to others paid to fake orgasms and pleasure. Role play is one thing, but if women are faking it, in whole or in part, all to seem like the person they believe their lovers want them to be, then it begs the question of who everyone is sleeping with – the person we know or the one they're pretending to be for our benefit because that's what they believe we want and, possibly, what we've come to believe we want, too.

So where does all this leave flashers? A sexual climate in which display is encouraged ought to be ideal for the flasher. Putting on a show is what it's all about. But there is a difference between a little role play and the flasher's display: one is a soft-core show in one's bedroom and the other is a full frontal one in public. That public tolerates, ignores or embraces the icons of lust that surround it. These images suggest sex, but it's an ignis fatuus, intended to show both the perfect sex symbols and the fact that it is unachievable either to be or bed them. Flashers, on the other hand, have no such subtlety. The closest they get to it is freeballing and cycling without knickers instead of just unzipping their trousers and lifting up their skirts. Their display doesn't suggest sex – it confronts the spectator with sex organs.

For the male flasher, this confrontation is a sexy experience, but for a culture in which that phallus and its magnificence are only suggested by images of women, gasping at the intensity of everything from shampoo and perfume to chocolate and alcohol, and no male image more graphic than the promising bulge of models' crotches, it is distasteful. It is also peculiar. Yes, a man can be bound-lessly enthusiastic about his penis, but that doesn't mean he can get it out in public. The only acceptable public displays of a penis are not the flesh itself but the suggestion of it and the invitation to use it by models, porn actresses, and the girls and women who buy into that image of sexiness. Male flashers discomfit because, instead of keeping their sexual practices in the bedroom, they take them out of it and impose them on others. Our soft porn culture might tell us what to want, but it imposes it upon us in a far more insidious fashion. The flasher is blatant: he gets off on showing you his penis whether you want to see it or not. And chances are, you won't. A lack of delight at the sight of a flasher's penis might be disappointing for him, but it takes only a glance to convince him that you are impressed. It may be delusional, but for a male flasher to be sated by a sexual encounter, that is all it takes. He will come, either at the scene or at home fantasizing about it, and that's all he desires. Though some flashers have partners, they tend to exist almost as an adjunct to flashing. They don't tell them they flash, they fantasize about flashing while having sex with them, and risk the loss of them in order to flash. When the urge to flash is upon them, nothing is more important. It is as intoxicating as the most potent drug, an all-consuming fixation that justifies the man's fetishization of his penis. He doesn't care that he's abnormal, a pervert, a freak – whatever people may call him. We can gasp and moan, faking it, trussed up like cheerleaders, our pores clogged with whipped cream and that's perfectly fine because we think that's what we want. In buying the products and image of sexiness, letting it become part of our self-perception, we've given our consent to the industry that created it. The flasher, on the other hand, asks no consent. Frequently, the less consenting the spectator the better. It is for this that he is punished by the legal and medical professions and by the society that surrounds him. This is why he is seen as a threat. Flashing, itself, is a pathetic act, but the man with penis in hand still has the power to threaten because we do not know what else he may do. If he enjoys forcing his penis upon a woman, what else might he enjoy doing without consent? No matter how light-heartedly he may say it is intended, the flasher is an imposition on our lives and on our selves. So long as we accept or fear this imposition, our lives are not truly our own. They belong, in part, to the flasher who believes he has a greater right to occupy the space around us than we do.

In a culture already inured to the display of women's bodies, the female flasher isn't as remarked on, nor is she considered a threat because she can't inflict any harm on those to whom she exposes her body. Like the male flasher, she believes she is desirable to all those she flashes. The men covet her in the flesh, she believes, and in chat room posts she is applauded, encouraged to reveal more, and told by men that they came thinking about her. She is a prize, a daring woman, sexy and desired. She doesn't need the accoutrements of romance or sexiness because she simply takes off her underwear. It's still an act, though, because she doesn't actually want to have sex with any of the men she flashes. She just wants to feel the rush of being looked at and wanted. She'll then escape to avoid being caught, either by the police or men at whom she has flashed. For all it is a public display, female flashing is a solitary activity: the woman wants the sexual gratification of being wanted, but from strangers rather than a partner. Even those who do it because their partners enjoy it are still flashing strangers. This desire to feel wanted yet not actually want to have sex with those who desire us is not limited to female flashers. It's more about projecting an image of sexiness than having sex. The difference between flashers and non-flashers is that the flasher's tease is blatantly sexual. It is also, very often, the basis of her self-esteem. Hence why she will take the risk of being caught or attacked, expose more and more of her body, and share her stories and pictures with fellow flashers in chat rooms. It's a precarious foundation on which to base one's self-perception, but though it would appear to be dependent on the response of men, it is actually based on what she reads into it. Like the male flasher, she assumes that any attention – even the merest glance – means men find her attractive and want her. She tries so hard to make herself attractive and convince herself that she is desirable, apparently unaware that the female body has become expendable to the point that, no matter how naked she may be, she is barely visible.

Acknowledgements

Thank you to everyone who took part in interviews and surveys for your thoughts and candid tales of your experiences. You were invaluable.

Thanks are due to all my friends (non-flashers as far as I'm aware) – in particular, John-Paul, Justin, and Martin – for remaining unflinching in the face of increasingly peculiar questions. An additional thank you to John-Paul for his great legal brain.

Thank you to Tariq Goddard at Zero Books for taking on the flashers and me, and for providing by far the most insightful, intelligent and helpful feedback I've ever received.

Finally, that flasher, whoever he was, who braved The Blitz with his torch and brought my grandparents together.

Biography

Kate Gould has a BA in Journalism and MA in Gender, Literature, and Modernity. She has worked as an editor, book critic, columnist, agent and publisher submissions assistant, magazine editor, reader for The Scotsman and Orange Short Story Prize, hotel critic, English language teacher, research assistant to Shere Hite and Germaine Greer, and ice cream vendor.

Now a writer and chief editorial consultant at The Fine Line Editorial Consultancy, she lives in Edinburgh with her pet rats, Georgia and Minnie.

Endnotes

1   BLAIR, David C. and LANYON, Richard I., "Exhibitionism: Etiology and Treatment", Psychological Bulletin, 89(3), 1981, pp439-463.
2   SNAITH, Philip, "Exhibitionism: a Clinical Conundrum", British Journal of Psychiatry, 143 (3), 1983, pp231-235.
3   COSTIN, Frank and DRAGUS, Juris, G., Abnormal Psychology: Patterns, Issues, Interventions (New York: Wiley, 1989), p.220.
4   REITZ, Willard and KEIL, William, "Behavioral Treatment of an Exhibitionist", in FISCHER, J., GOCHROS, H., Handbook of Behavior Therapy with Sexual Problems, Vol. II: Approaches to Specific Problems (New York: Pergamon Press, 1977) pp485-488.
5   ROSEN, Ismond, "Perversion as a Regulatory of Self-Esteem", in ROSEN, Ismond, ed., Sexual Deviation (Oxford: Oxford University Press, 1979) pp65-78.
6   CARLISLE, J., MCGUIRE, R. J. and YOUNG, B., "Sexual Deviations as Conditioned Behaviour: a Hypothesis", Behavior Research and Therapy, 2, 1965, pp185-190.
7   Ibid.
8   FELDMAN, M., P., MACCULOCH M., J., MELLOR, V., and PINSCHOF J., M., "The Application of Anticipatory Avoidance Learning to the Treatment of Homosexuality, III. The Sexual Orientation Method", Behaviour Research and Therapy, 4, 1966, pp289-299.
9   MACCULLOCH, M., J., WILLIAMS, C., and BIRTLES, C., J., "The Successful Application of Aversion Therapy to an Adolescent Exhibitionist", in WOLFE, J. and

REYNA, L., J., eds, Behaviour Therapy in Psychiatric Practice (New York: Pergamon Press, 1976) pp71-76.

10 MALETZKY, Barry, "'Assisted' Covert Sensitization in the Treatment of Exhibitionism", Journal of Consulting and Clinical Psychology, 42 (1), 1974, pp34-40.

11 JONES, I. H. and FREI, D., "Provoked Anxiety as a Treatment of Exhibitionism", British Journal of Psychiatry, 131 (3), 1977, pp295-300.

12 Ibid.

13 REITZ, Willard and KEIL, William, "Behavioral Treatment of an Exhibitionist", in FISCHER, J., GOCHROS, H., Handbook of Behavior Therapy with Sexual Problems, Vol. II: Approaches to Specific Problems (New York: Pergamon Press, 1977) pp485-488.

14 SNAITH, R., P., and COLLINS, S., A., "Five Exhibitionists and a Method of Treatment", British Journal of Psychiatry 138 (2), 1981, pp126-130.
    CARLISLE, J., MCGUIRE, R. J. and YOUNG, B., "Sexual Deviations as Conditioned Behaviour: a Hypothesis", Behavior Research and Therapy, 2, 1965, pp185-190.

15 JONES, I. H. and FREI, D., "Provoked Anxiety as a Treatment of Exhibitionism", British Journal of Psychiatry, 131 (3), 1977, pp295-300.

16 See, for example, EVANS, John, "Exhibitionism", in COSTELLO, Charles, ed., Symptoms of Psychopathology: A Handbook (New York: John Wiley & Sons, 1970) pp560-573.
    LASCHET, U., "Antiandrogen in the Treatment of Sex Offenders: Modes of Action and Therapeutic Outcome", in ZUBIN, J., and MONEY, J., eds, Contemporary Sexual Behavior: Critical Issues In The 1970s (Baltimore: John Hopkins University Press, 1973).

MONEY, J., "Use of Androgen-depleting Hormones in the Treatment of Male Sex Offenders", Journal of Sex Research, 6, 1970, pp165-172.

WALKER, P., A., "The Role of Antiandrogens in the Treatment of Sex Offenders", in QUALLS, C., B., WINCZE, J., P., and BARLOW, D., H., eds, The Prevention of Sexual Disorders: Issues and Approaches (New York: Plenum Press, 1978).

17 HOUSE OF LORDS HANSARD WRITTEN ANSWERS, 9 February 2000, Column WA87.

18 GROB, Charles, S., "Single Case Study: Female Exhibitionism", The Journal of Nervous and Mental Disease, 173 (4), 1985, pp253-256.

19 Ibid., p.255.

20 Ibid., p.256.

21 Ibid., p.256.

22 O'CONNOR, Art, A., "Female Sex Offenders", British Journal of Psychiatry, 150 (5), 1987, pp615-620.

23 WESTE, Richard, The Book of Demeanor and the Allowance and Disallowance of Certaine Misdemeanors in Companie (1619) quoted in ELIAS Norbert, The Civilizing Process: The History of Manners, trans., JEPHCOTT, Edmund (New York: Urizen Books, 1978) pp131-132.

24 LASEGUE, Ernest Charles, "Les Exhibitionistes", L'Union Medicale, Troisieme Serie, 23, 1877, pp709-714.

25 PARLIAMENTARY DEBATES, N. S. (London: TC Hansard).
Vol. 4 1821
Vol. 5 1821
Vol. 6 1822
Vol. 10 1824
Vol. 11 1824

26 VAGRANCY ACT (1824, section 4) in The Statutes Revisited, 3 Geo. IV to 5&6 Will. IV, vol. 3, 1822-1835 (London: His Majesty's Stationary Office, 1950).

27 Town Police Clauses Act (1847, section 28).

28 Army Act (1881), information licensed under the terms of the Open Government Licence, legislation.gov.uk.

29 CRIMINAL JUSTICE ACT (1925, section 42), in PUBLIC GENERAL ACTS AND MEASURES OF 1925, vol. 2, 15&16 Geo. 5 (London: Coding, The King's Printer of Acts of Parliament, 1925).

30 PUBLIC ORDER ACT (1986, section 5(1)) in Public Acts and Measures of 1986, 4 Elizabeth II (London: Her Majesty's Stationary Office, 1987).

31 THE REPORT OF A HOWARD LEAGUE WORKING PARTY, Unlawful Sex: Offences, Victims and Offenders in the Criminal Justice System of England and Wales (London: Waterlow Publishers Ltd, 1985).

32 Regina v Lunderbech (1991), LR. 784.

33 Regina v Farrell (1862), 9 Cox CC 446.

34 Regina v Mayling (1963), 2QB717.

35 Knuller v DPP (1972), AC435.

36 Regina v Wellard (1884), 14QBD63.

37 Regina v Walker (1996), 14QBD63.

38 Regina v Elliot and White (1861), 169 Eng. Rep. 1332.

39 Sexual Offences Act (2003, section 66), information licensed under the terms of the Open Government Licence, legislation.gov.uk.

40 Sexual Offences (Scotland) Act (2009, section 8), information licensed under the terms of the Open Government Licence, legislation.gov.uk.

41 Ibid.

42 Sexual Offences Act (2003, section 66), information licensed under the terms of the Open Government Licence, legislation.gov.uk.

GREAT BRITAIN HOUSE OF COMMONS JOURNALS
Vol. 76 Session 1821
Vol. 77 Session 1822
Vol. 79 Session 1824
The All England Law Reports, vol. 1 (London: Butterworths, 1936-1989)
THE INCORPORATED COUNCIL OF LAW REPORTING FOR ENGLAND AND WALES, The Law Reports, Queen's Bench Division, vol. 2 (London: 1963)

Contemporary culture has eliminated both the concept of the public and the figure of the intellectual. Former public spaces – both physical and cultural – are now either derelict or colonized by advertising. A cretinous anti-intellectualism presides, cheerled by expensively educated hacks in the pay of multinational corporations who reassure their bored readers that there is no need to rouse themselves from their interpassive stupor. The informal censorship internalized and propagated by the cultural workers of late capitalism generates a banal conformity that the propaganda chiefs of Stalinism could only ever have dreamt of imposing. Zer0 Books knows that another kind of discourse – intellectual without being academic, popular without being populist – is not only possible: it is already flourishing, in the regions beyond the striplit malls of so-called mass media and the neurotically bureaucratic halls of the academy. Zer0 is committed to the idea of publishing as a making public of the intellectual. It is convinced that in the unthinking, blandly consensual culture in which we live, critical and engaged theoretical reflection is more important than ever before.